COUNTRIES IN THE NEWS

SAUDI ARABIA

Kieran Walsh

Rourke

Publishing LLC

Vero Beach, Florida 32964

www.rourkepublishing.com

The country's flag is correct at the time of going to press.

PHOTO CREDITS:
Cover, pages 4, 8, 15, 17, and 18 © Getty Images; pages 9, 12, and 13 © Peter Langer Associated Media Group; pages 6 and 10 © PhotoDisc, Inc.

Title page: Camels are a common sight in Saudi Arabia.

Editor: Frank Sloan

Cover and interior design by Nicola Stratford

Library of Congress Cataloging-in-Publication Data

Walsh, Kieran.
    Saudi Arabia / Kieran Walsh.
        p. cm. — (Countries in the news)
    Includes bibliographical references and index.
    Contents: Welcome to Saudi Arabia — The people — Life in Saudi Arabia — School and sports — Food and holidays — The future — Fast facts — The Muslim world.
    ISBN 1-58952-681-3
    1. Saudi Arabia—Juvenile literature.   [1. Saudi Arabia.]
I. Title. II. Series: Walsh, Kieran. Countries in the news.

DS204.25.W35 2003
953.8—dc21   2003005895

Printed in the USA

CG/CG

TABLE OF CONTENTS

WELCOME TO
SAUDI ARABIA

Saudi Arabia is a large country in southwest Asia. It covers most of the Arabian **peninsula** between the Red Sea, the Indian Ocean, and the Persian Gulf.

The country is shaped roughly like a triangle. Saudi Arabia is about 1,290 miles (2,076 kilometers) across at its widest point.

A modern look along the beach in Jedda

4

It is about the same size as the state of Alaska or the country of Mexico.

Much of Saudi Arabia is dry, and most of the land is desert.

There is much sand and very little rain throughout the country. Although it is hot during the day, at night in some places there can even be **frost**. There are a few mountains along the west coast.

Buried under all the sand is the richest supply of oil in the world. All this oil has made Saudi Arabia a wealthy and powerful country.

The kingdom of Saudi Arabia was founded in 1927. The royal capital of the country is Riyadh, but Jedda is where the government meets.

The most important city, however, in Saudi Arabia is **Mecca**. This is the **Muslims'** holy city. It is believed that **Muhammad**, the founder of **Islam**, was born there. Most Muslims pray several times a day. And when they do, they face toward Mecca.

Each year several million **pilgrims** visit Mecca. They go there because it is a holy place. The trip to Mecca is known as the **hajj**.

6

Oil is Saudi Arabia's most important natural resource.

THE PEOPLE

Most of the people of Saudi Arabia are Arabs. They speak the Arabic language. Most Saudis are Muslims. This means they follow the religion of Islam.

In Saudi Arabia, more people are beginning to live in cities. And the cities are constantly growing.

The Saudi king (seated, at left) greets the king of Jordan.

8

Bedouin men by the roadside

However, many are still **nomads** known as **Bedouin**. They spend their time looking for food for their animals. They live in black tents made of animal hair.

9

Some Saudis work in the oil industry. And some work in other industries. However, three out of five people are farmers. Where there is water, it is easy to grow crops. Even in the desert, there are **oases**, where water from under the ground comes to the surface. Oases often feature palm trees, where dates and figs are grown. Fishing is important in the Persian Gulf.

Palm trees tower above an oasis.

LIFE IN
SAUDI ARABIA

Men in Saudi Arabia between the ages of 18 and 35 must serve in the military. Most Saudi men wear traditional robes and headgear.

A Saudi Arabian sports traditional headgear.

In cities women wear black veils over their clothes. And they do not drive cars! Some women still cover their faces when they go out in public. But more and more, women are not following this old custom.

12

A veiled woman is a common sight in Saudi Arabia.

SCHOOL AND SPORTS

By law, children do not have to go to school. There are many new schools, most of which are free. Most of them are run by the government. Until recently, only boys attended school, but now more girls are going to them. Boys and girls still attend separate schools. There are some colleges and universities in Saudi Arabia, but many people go to other countries for their college education.

! Soccer is the most popular team sport in Saudi Arabia. Volleyball, basketball, and tennis are also played there. Water sports are enjoyed along the country's coastlines.

Saudi boys enjoy a day out in Jedda.

FOOD AND HOLIDAYS

Saudi Arabia grows very few crops that can be used as food. Most of the food eaten in Saudi Arabia comes from other countries. A typical meal consists of lamb or chicken served over flavored rice. Most people eat with their hands while sitting on the floor. Coffee and tea are popular beverages.

The best-known Muslim holiday is the month of **Ramadan**. During this time, Muslims cannot eat or drink during the day, so they **fast**. At the end of Ramadan, they celebrate the feast of **Id ul Fitr**.

The U.S. president entertains a Saudi prince at a White House Ramadan dinner.

The old and the new: a man in traditional Saudi dress walks past an oil refinery.

THE FUTURE

Oil makes Saudi Arabia a very rich country. And Saudis are using much of the money from the sale of oil to develop industry in their country.

But only water will make crops grow. New dams supply water for farms. Factories have been built that take salt water from the sea and turn it into fresh water. This water can be used to **irrigate** crops.

Even many of today's Bedouin live modern lives. They often drive SUVs instead of riding on camels, the traditional Saudi Arabian "ship of the desert."

FAST FACTS

Area: 830,000 square miles
(2,149,534 square kilometers)

Borders: Kuwait, Iraq, Jordan, Yemen, Oman,
United Arab Republic, Qatar

Population: 23,513,330
Monetary Unit: riyal

Largest Cities: Riyadh (4,761,000);
Jedda (3,192,000); Mecca(1,335,000)
Government: Monarchy

Religion: 100% Muslims
Crops: dates, meat, barley, tomatoes

Natural Resources: oil, gas, gold, copper, iron
Major Industries: oil, oil products

20

THE MUSLIM WORLD

There are more than 1,200,000,000 Muslims in the world. Almost two thirds of them live in Asia and Africa. There are two major groups of Muslims: 16% of them are Shiites and 83% are known as Sunni.

Muslims follow the Islam religion. Muslims believe in God, who they know as Allah. The religion was begun around AD 610 when Muhammad became known as a prophet. He wrote down his teachings in a holy book called the Koran.

In AD 622 Muhammad fled from Mecca to Medina, which is about 200 miles (320 kilometers) north of Mecca. The Islamic calendar, which is a lunar calendar, dates from this time.

GLOSSARY

Bedouin (BED oo in) — kinds of nomads who wander in the deserts

fast (FAST) — to go without food, usually for religious reasons

frost (FROHST) — ice that may cover some mountainous areas

hajj (HODGE) — a trip to Mecca made by Muslims

Id ul Fitr (ID UHL FIT ur) — a holiday celebrated at the end of Ramadan

irrigate (ir uh GAYT) — to provide water for growing crops

Islam (IZ lahm) — the religion followed by Muslims

Mecca (MECK uh) — the Muslim holy city of Saudi Arabia

Muhammad (muh HAM mud) — a prophet, thought by many to be the founder of the religion of Islam

Muslims (MUZ lumz) — people who follow the religion of Islam

nomads (NOH madz) — wanderers who follow their livestock through desert regions

oases (oh ACE eez) — wet places in deserts where water can be found

peninsula (puh NIN suh luh) — a piece of land that is surrounded by water on three of its four sides

pilgrims (PILL GRIMZ) — travelers who make a special journey to a place

Ramadan (RAM uh DAN) — the ninth month of the Muslim year

22

FURTHER READING

Find out more about Saudi Arabia with these helpful books:

- Balcavage, Dynise. *Saudi Arabia.* Gareth Stevens, 2001.
- Fazio, Wende. *Saudi Arabia.* Gareth Stevens, 2000.
- Marchant, Kerena. *Muslim Festival Tales.* Raintree Steck Vaughn, 2001.
- Temple, Bob. *Saudi Arabia.* Child's World, 2001.

WEBSITE TO VISIT

- www.saudiembassy.net/

INDEX

About the Author

Kieran Walsh is a writer of children's nonfiction books, primarily on historical and social studies topics. A graduate of Manhattan College, in Riverdale, NY, his degree is in Communications. Walsh has been involved in the children's book field as editor, proofreader, and illustrator as well as author.